50 Cheap Eats Recipes for Home

By: Kelly Johnson

Table of Contents

- One-Pot Pasta Primavera
- Chickpea Stir-Fry
- Vegetable Fried Rice
- Lentil Soup
- Baked Potato Bar
- Cabbage and Sausage Skillet
- Stuffed Bell Peppers
- Spaghetti Aglio e Olio
- Tomato and Basil Bruschetta
- Black Bean Tacos
- Egg Fried Rice
- Vegetable Curry
- Homemade Vegetable Soup
- Quesadillas with Cheese and Beans
- Tuna Pasta Salad
- Potato and Leek Soup
- Pancakes with Fruit
- Sweet Potato Hash
- Cabbage Roll Casserole
- Homemade Pizza with Seasonal Veggies
- Chicken and Rice Casserole
- Zucchini Noodles with Marinara
- Sloppy Joes
- Garlic Butter Shrimp and Rice
- Baked Ziti
- Macaroni and Cheese
- Curried Lentil Salad
- Broccoli and Cheese Stuffed Chicken
- Veggie Frittata
- Pasta Salad with Veggies
- Eggplant Parmesan
- Chickpea Salad Sandwich
- Creamy Tomato Soup
- Cauliflower Tacos
- Sweet Potato and Black Bean Chili

- Rice and Beans
- Spinach and Cheese Stuffed Shells
- Slaw Tacos
- Roasted Vegetable Quinoa Bowl
- Creamy Mushroom Risotto
- Garlic Roasted Chickpeas
- Cabbage Stir-Fry
- Beet and Goat Cheese Salad
- Cheesy Broccoli Casserole
- Grilled Cheese with Tomato Soup
- Shrimp and Grits
- Veggie Burrito Bowls
- Pesto Pasta with Peas
- Baked Ratatouille
- Overnight Oats with Fruits

One-Pot Pasta Primavera

Ingredients

- 12 oz pasta (e.g., penne or fusilli)
- 2 cups vegetable broth
- 1 cup cherry tomatoes, halved
- 1 bell pepper, sliced
- 1 zucchini, sliced
- 1 cup broccoli florets
- 2 cloves garlic, minced
- 2 tablespoons olive oil
- 1 teaspoon Italian seasoning
- Salt and pepper to taste
- Grated Parmesan cheese for serving (optional)

Instructions

1. In a large pot, heat olive oil over medium heat. Add garlic and sauté for about 1 minute until fragrant.
2. Add the pasta, vegetable broth, cherry tomatoes, bell pepper, zucchini, broccoli, Italian seasoning, salt, and pepper.
3. Bring to a boil, then reduce heat and simmer for 10-12 minutes, stirring occasionally, until the pasta is cooked and the liquid is mostly absorbed.
4. Serve warm, topped with grated Parmesan cheese if desired.

Chickpea Stir-Fry

Ingredients

- 1 can (15 oz) chickpeas, drained and rinsed
- 2 cups mixed vegetables (e.g., bell peppers, broccoli, carrots)
- 2 tablespoons soy sauce
- 1 tablespoon olive oil
- 1 tablespoon ginger, minced
- 2 cloves garlic, minced
- Cooked rice or quinoa for serving

Instructions

1. In a large skillet, heat olive oil over medium heat. Add ginger and garlic, cooking for about 1 minute until fragrant.
2. Add mixed vegetables and sauté for 5-7 minutes until tender.
3. Stir in chickpeas and soy sauce, cooking for an additional 3-4 minutes until heated through.
4. Serve over cooked rice or quinoa.

Vegetable Fried Rice

Ingredients

- 3 cups cooked rice (preferably day-old)
- 1 cup mixed vegetables (e.g., peas, carrots, bell peppers)
- 2 tablespoons soy sauce
- 2 eggs, beaten
- 2 tablespoons sesame oil or vegetable oil
- 2 green onions, chopped
- Salt and pepper to taste

Instructions

1. In a large skillet or wok, heat sesame oil over medium-high heat. Add beaten eggs and scramble until fully cooked. Remove from the skillet and set aside.
2. In the same skillet, add mixed vegetables and stir-fry for 3-4 minutes until tender.
3. Add cooked rice, soy sauce, and the scrambled eggs back into the skillet. Stir well to combine, heating through. Season with salt, pepper, and green onions before serving.

Lentil Soup

Ingredients

- 1 cup lentils (green or brown), rinsed
- 1 onion, diced
- 2 carrots, diced
- 2 celery stalks, diced
- 2 cloves garlic, minced
- 4 cups vegetable broth
- 1 can (14 oz) diced tomatoes
- 1 teaspoon thyme
- Salt and pepper to taste
- 2 tablespoons olive oil

Instructions

1. In a large pot, heat olive oil over medium heat. Sauté onion, carrots, and celery until softened, about 5-7 minutes. Add garlic and cook for an additional minute.
2. Add lentils, vegetable broth, diced tomatoes, thyme, salt, and pepper. Bring to a boil, then reduce heat and simmer for 25-30 minutes until lentils are tender.
3. Adjust seasoning as needed and serve warm.

Baked Potato Bar

Ingredients

- 4 large russet potatoes
- Toppings (choose your favorites):
    - Sour cream
    - Shredded cheese
    - Chives
    - Bacon bits
    - Steamed broccoli
    - Chili
    - Butter

Instructions

1. Preheat oven to 425°F (220°C). Pierce each potato several times with a fork.
2. Bake potatoes directly on the oven rack for 45-60 minutes, until tender.
3. Let cool slightly, then cut open and fluff the insides with a fork. Set up a toppings bar and let everyone customize their potatoes.

Cabbage and Sausage Skillet

Ingredients

- 1 lb smoked sausage, sliced
- 1 small head green cabbage, chopped
- 1 onion, sliced
- 2 cloves garlic, minced
- 2 tablespoons olive oil
- Salt and pepper to taste
- 1 teaspoon paprika (optional)

Instructions

1. In a large skillet, heat olive oil over medium heat. Add sliced sausage and cook until browned, about 5-7 minutes.
2. Add onion and garlic, cooking until onion is translucent.
3. Stir in cabbage, salt, pepper, and paprika. Cook, stirring occasionally, until cabbage is wilted and tender, about 10-15 minutes. Serve warm.

Stuffed Bell Peppers

Ingredients

- 4 bell peppers, tops removed and seeds discarded
- 1 cup cooked rice
- 1 can (15 oz) black beans, drained and rinsed
- 1 cup corn (fresh or frozen)
- 1 cup salsa
- 1 teaspoon cumin
- 1 teaspoon chili powder
- 1 cup shredded cheese (optional)

Instructions

1. Preheat oven to 375°F (190°C). Arrange the bell peppers in a baking dish.
2. In a bowl, combine cooked rice, black beans, corn, salsa, cumin, chili powder, and half of the cheese if using.
3. Stuff each pepper with the mixture and top with remaining cheese. Cover with foil and bake for 30-35 minutes, removing foil for the last 10 minutes to brown the cheese.

Spaghetti Aglio e Olio

Ingredients

- 12 oz spaghetti
- 6 cloves garlic, thinly sliced
- ½ cup olive oil
- 1 teaspoon red pepper flakes (adjust to taste)
- Salt to taste
- Fresh parsley, chopped for garnish
- Grated Parmesan cheese for serving (optional)

Instructions

1. Cook spaghetti according to package instructions in salted water. Reserve ½ cup pasta water before draining.
2. In a large skillet, heat olive oil over medium heat. Add sliced garlic and red pepper flakes, cooking until garlic is golden (about 2-3 minutes).
3. Add the drained spaghetti to the skillet, tossing to coat in the oil. If needed, add reserved pasta water for moisture.
4. Season with salt and garnish with chopped parsley and Parmesan cheese if desired. Serve immediately.

Tomato and Basil Bruschetta

Ingredients

- 1 baguette, sliced
- 3 cups ripe tomatoes, diced
- 1 cup fresh basil, chopped
- 2 cloves garlic, minced
- 3 tablespoons olive oil
- Salt and pepper to taste
- Balsamic glaze for drizzling (optional)

Instructions

1. Preheat oven to 400°F (200°C). Arrange baguette slices on a baking sheet and brush with olive oil. Toast in the oven for about 5-7 minutes until golden.
2. In a bowl, combine diced tomatoes, basil, garlic, olive oil, salt, and pepper. Let sit for 10 minutes to allow flavors to meld.
3. Spoon the tomato mixture onto toasted baguette slices and drizzle with balsamic glaze if desired. Serve immediately.

Black Bean Tacos

Ingredients

- 1 can (15 oz) black beans, drained and rinsed
- 1 teaspoon cumin
- 1 teaspoon chili powder
- Salt and pepper to taste
- 8 corn tortillas
- Toppings: diced avocado, salsa, chopped cilantro, lime wedges

Instructions

1. In a saucepan, heat black beans over medium heat. Add cumin, chili powder, salt, and pepper. Cook until heated through, about 5 minutes.
2. Warm tortillas in a skillet or microwave.
3. Assemble tacos by filling each tortilla with black beans and your choice of toppings. Serve with lime wedges.

Egg Fried Rice

Ingredients

- 3 cups cooked rice (preferably day-old)
- 3 eggs, beaten
- 1 cup mixed vegetables (e.g., peas, carrots, corn)
- 3 green onions, chopped
- 3 tablespoons soy sauce
- 2 tablespoons vegetable oil
- Salt and pepper to taste

Instructions

1. Heat 1 tablespoon of oil in a large skillet or wok over medium heat. Add beaten eggs, scrambling until fully cooked. Remove and set aside.
2. Add remaining oil to the skillet. Stir-fry mixed vegetables for 3-4 minutes until tender.
3. Add cooked rice, soy sauce, and scrambled eggs. Stir well to combine, seasoning with salt and pepper. Cook for another 2-3 minutes. Serve warm.

Vegetable Curry

Ingredients

- 2 tablespoons vegetable oil
- 1 onion, diced
- 2 cloves garlic, minced
- 1 tablespoon ginger, minced
- 2 cups mixed vegetables (e.g., bell peppers, carrots, peas)
- 1 can (14 oz) coconut milk
- 2 tablespoons curry powder
- Salt to taste
- Fresh cilantro for garnish

Instructions

1. In a large pot, heat oil over medium heat. Sauté onion until translucent, about 5 minutes. Add garlic and ginger, cooking for an additional minute.
2. Add mixed vegetables and curry powder, stirring to coat. Cook for 3-4 minutes.
3. Pour in coconut milk, bring to a simmer, and cook for 15-20 minutes until vegetables are tender. Season with salt and garnish with cilantro before serving.

Homemade Vegetable Soup

Ingredients

- 2 tablespoons olive oil
- 1 onion, diced
- 2 carrots, diced
- 2 celery stalks, diced
- 2 cloves garlic, minced
- 4 cups vegetable broth
- 2 cups mixed vegetables (e.g., green beans, zucchini, corn)
- 1 can (14 oz) diced tomatoes
- 1 teaspoon thyme
- Salt and pepper to taste

Instructions

1. In a large pot, heat olive oil over medium heat. Sauté onion, carrots, and celery until softened, about 5-7 minutes. Add garlic and cook for another minute.
2. Add vegetable broth, mixed vegetables, diced tomatoes, thyme, salt, and pepper. Bring to a boil, then reduce heat and simmer for 20-25 minutes until vegetables are tender. Serve warm.

Quesadillas with Cheese and Beans

Ingredients

- 8 flour tortillas
- 1 can (15 oz) black beans, drained and rinsed
- 2 cups shredded cheese (e.g., cheddar, Monterey Jack)
- 1 teaspoon cumin
- 1 teaspoon chili powder
- Olive oil for cooking
- Salsa and sour cream for serving

Instructions

1. In a bowl, combine black beans, cumin, and chili powder. Mash slightly with a fork.
2. Heat a skillet over medium heat and brush with olive oil. Place one tortilla in the skillet, sprinkle half with cheese, top with bean mixture, and fold the other half over.
3. Cook until golden and crispy on both sides, about 3-4 minutes per side. Repeat with remaining tortillas. Cut into wedges and serve with salsa and sour cream.

Tuna Pasta Salad

Ingredients

- 8 oz pasta (e.g., rotini or macaroni)
- 1 can (5 oz) tuna, drained
- 1 cup frozen peas, thawed
- ½ cup mayonnaise
- 1 tablespoon Dijon mustard
- Salt and pepper to taste
- 1 tablespoon lemon juice
- Chopped parsley for garnish

Instructions

1. Cook pasta according to package instructions. Drain and rinse with cold water.
2. In a large bowl, combine cooked pasta, tuna, peas, mayonnaise, mustard, salt, pepper, and lemon juice. Mix until well combined.
3. Garnish with chopped parsley and serve chilled or at room temperature.

Potato and Leek Soup

Ingredients

- 2 tablespoons butter
- 1 onion, diced
- 2 leeks, sliced and cleaned
- 4 medium potatoes, peeled and diced
- 4 cups vegetable broth
- Salt and pepper to taste
- 1 cup heavy cream (optional)
- Chopped chives for garnish

Instructions

1. In a large pot, melt butter over medium heat. Add onion and leeks, cooking until softened, about 5-7 minutes.
2. Add diced potatoes and vegetable broth. Bring to a boil, then reduce heat and simmer for 20-25 minutes until potatoes are tender.
3. Use an immersion blender to blend until smooth (or blend in batches in a regular blender). Stir in heavy cream if using, and season with salt and pepper. Garnish with chives before serving.

Pancakes with Fruit

Ingredients

- 1 cup all-purpose flour
- 2 tablespoons sugar
- 1 teaspoon baking powder
- ½ teaspoon baking soda
- ¼ teaspoon salt
- 1 cup buttermilk
- 1 large egg
- 2 tablespoons melted butter
- Fresh fruit (e.g., berries, banana slices) for topping
- Maple syrup for serving

Instructions

1. In a bowl, whisk together flour, sugar, baking powder, baking soda, and salt.
2. In another bowl, mix buttermilk, egg, and melted butter. Combine wet and dry ingredients until just mixed.
3. Heat a non-stick skillet over medium heat. Pour ¼ cup of batter for each pancake, cooking until bubbles form, then flip and cook until golden. Serve with fresh fruit and maple syrup.

Sweet Potato Hash

Ingredients

- 2 medium sweet potatoes, diced
- 1 bell pepper, diced
- 1 onion, diced
- 2 tablespoons olive oil
- 1 teaspoon paprika
- Salt and pepper to taste
- 2 eggs (optional)

Instructions

1. In a large skillet, heat olive oil over medium heat. Add diced sweet potatoes and cook for about 10 minutes, stirring occasionally, until they start to soften.
2. Add bell pepper and onion, cooking for an additional 5-7 minutes until all vegetables are tender. Season with paprika, salt, and pepper.
3. If desired, make two wells in the hash and crack an egg into each. Cover and cook until eggs are set. Serve warm.

Cabbage Roll Casserole

Ingredients

- 1 lb ground beef or turkey
- 1 onion, diced
- 1 small head cabbage, chopped
- 1 can (15 oz) tomato sauce
- 1 cup cooked rice
- 1 teaspoon garlic powder
- Salt and pepper to taste
- 1 teaspoon Italian seasoning
- ½ cup shredded cheese (optional)

Instructions

1. Preheat oven to 350°F (175°C). In a large skillet, brown the ground meat with onion until cooked through. Drain excess fat.
2. In a large bowl, combine cooked meat mixture, chopped cabbage, tomato sauce, cooked rice, garlic powder, salt, pepper, and Italian seasoning.
3. Transfer the mixture to a greased baking dish. Cover with foil and bake for 45 minutes. If using cheese, uncover and sprinkle on top, baking for an additional 10 minutes until melted.

Homemade Pizza with Seasonal Veggies

Ingredients

- 1 pre-made pizza crust
- ½ cup pizza sauce
- 1 ½ cups shredded mozzarella cheese
- 1 cup seasonal veggies (e.g., zucchini, bell peppers, mushrooms)
- 1 teaspoon Italian seasoning
- Olive oil for drizzling

Instructions

1. Preheat oven according to pizza crust package instructions.
2. Roll out the pizza crust and place it on a baking sheet. Spread pizza sauce evenly over the crust.
3. Sprinkle mozzarella cheese on top, then arrange seasonal veggies. Sprinkle with Italian seasoning and drizzle with olive oil.
4. Bake according to crust instructions or until the cheese is bubbly and golden. Let cool slightly before slicing.

Chicken and Rice Casserole

Ingredients

- 2 cups cooked chicken, shredded
- 1 cup uncooked rice
- 2 cups chicken broth
- 1 cup frozen mixed vegetables
- 1 can (10.5 oz) cream of mushroom soup
- 1 teaspoon garlic powder
- Salt and pepper to taste
- ½ cup shredded cheese (optional)

Instructions

1. Preheat oven to 375°F (190°C). In a large bowl, mix chicken, rice, chicken broth, mixed vegetables, cream of mushroom soup, garlic powder, salt, and pepper.
2. Pour the mixture into a greased baking dish. Cover with foil and bake for 45-50 minutes, or until rice is tender.
3. If using cheese, uncover and sprinkle on top, baking for an additional 10 minutes until melted.

Zucchini Noodles with Marinara

Ingredients

- 2 medium zucchini, spiralized
- 2 cups marinara sauce
- 2 tablespoons olive oil
- 2 cloves garlic, minced
- Salt and pepper to taste
- Grated Parmesan cheese for serving (optional)

Instructions

1. In a large skillet, heat olive oil over medium heat. Add garlic and sauté for about 1 minute until fragrant.
2. Add spiralized zucchini and sauté for 2-3 minutes until just tender. Season with salt and pepper.
3. Pour marinara sauce over the zucchini noodles and stir to combine. Heat through and serve topped with Parmesan cheese if desired.

Sloppy Joes

Ingredients

- 1 lb ground beef or turkey
- 1 onion, diced
- 1 bell pepper, diced
- 1 cup ketchup
- 2 tablespoons Worcestershire sauce
- 1 tablespoon brown sugar
- Salt and pepper to taste
- Burger buns for serving

Instructions

1. In a skillet, brown ground meat with onion and bell pepper over medium heat. Drain excess fat.
2. Stir in ketchup, Worcestershire sauce, brown sugar, salt, and pepper. Simmer for 5-10 minutes until thickened.
3. Serve the mixture on burger buns.

Garlic Butter Shrimp and Rice

Ingredients

- 1 lb shrimp, peeled and deveined
- 2 cups cooked rice
- 4 tablespoons butter
- 4 cloves garlic, minced
- 1 tablespoon lemon juice
- Salt and pepper to taste
- Chopped parsley for garnish

Instructions

1. In a large skillet, melt butter over medium heat. Add garlic and sauté for 1 minute until fragrant.
2. Add shrimp and cook for 2-3 minutes on each side until pink and opaque. Stir in lemon juice, salt, and pepper.
3. Serve the shrimp over cooked rice, garnished with chopped parsley.

Baked Ziti

Ingredients

- 12 oz ziti pasta
- 2 cups marinara sauce
- 2 cups ricotta cheese
- 2 cups shredded mozzarella cheese
- ½ cup grated Parmesan cheese
- 1 teaspoon Italian seasoning
- Salt and pepper to taste

Instructions

1. Preheat oven to 375°F (190°C). Cook ziti according to package instructions; drain.
2. In a large bowl, combine cooked ziti, marinara sauce, ricotta cheese, half of the mozzarella, Italian seasoning, salt, and pepper.
3. Transfer to a greased baking dish and top with remaining mozzarella and Parmesan. Bake for 25-30 minutes until bubbly and golden.

Macaroni and Cheese

Ingredients

- 8 oz elbow macaroni
- 2 tablespoons butter
- 2 tablespoons all-purpose flour
- 2 cups milk
- 2 cups shredded cheese (e.g., cheddar, Monterey Jack)
- Salt and pepper to taste
- Breadcrumbs for topping (optional)

Instructions

1. Cook macaroni according to package instructions; drain.
2. In a saucepan, melt butter over medium heat. Whisk in flour and cook for 1 minute. Gradually add milk, stirring until thickened.
3. Stir in cheese until melted. Combine with cooked macaroni and season with salt and pepper.
4. Pour into a greased baking dish. If desired, sprinkle breadcrumbs on top. Bake at 350°F (175°C) for 20-25 minutes until golden and bubbly.

Curried Lentil Salad

Ingredients

- 1 cup lentils, rinsed
- 3 cups vegetable broth
- 1 cup diced bell peppers
- 1 cup diced cucumber
- ½ cup red onion, diced
- ½ cup fresh cilantro, chopped
- 2 tablespoons olive oil
- 2 tablespoons apple cider vinegar
- 1 tablespoon curry powder
- Salt and pepper to taste

Instructions

1. In a saucepan, combine lentils and vegetable broth. Bring to a boil, then reduce heat and simmer for 20-25 minutes until tender. Drain and let cool.
2. In a large bowl, combine cooled lentils, bell peppers, cucumber, red onion, and cilantro.
3. In a small bowl, whisk together olive oil, apple cider vinegar, curry powder, salt, and pepper. Pour over the salad and toss to combine. Serve chilled or at room temperature.

Broccoli and Cheese Stuffed Chicken

Ingredients

- 4 boneless, skinless chicken breasts
- 1 cup broccoli florets, steamed and chopped
- 1 cup shredded cheddar cheese
- 1 teaspoon garlic powder
- Salt and pepper to taste
- 2 tablespoons olive oil

Instructions

1. Preheat oven to 375°F (190°C). In a bowl, mix chopped broccoli, cheddar cheese, garlic powder, salt, and pepper.
2. Cut a pocket into each chicken breast and stuff with the broccoli and cheese mixture.
3. Heat olive oil in a skillet over medium heat. Sear the chicken breasts for 3-4 minutes on each side until golden.
4. Transfer chicken to a baking dish and bake for 20-25 minutes until cooked through. Serve warm.

Veggie Frittata

Ingredients

- 6 large eggs
- 1 cup milk
- 1 cup mixed vegetables (e.g., spinach, bell peppers, onions)
- ½ cup shredded cheese (e.g., feta or cheddar)
- Salt and pepper to taste
- 2 tablespoons olive oil

Instructions

1. Preheat oven to 375°F (190°C). In a bowl, whisk together eggs, milk, salt, and pepper.
2. In an oven-safe skillet, heat olive oil over medium heat. Sauté mixed vegetables until tender.
3. Pour the egg mixture over the vegetables and cook until edges begin to set, about 5 minutes.
4. Sprinkle cheese on top and transfer to the oven. Bake for 15-20 minutes until the frittata is set. Slice and serve warm.

Pasta Salad with Veggies

Ingredients

- 8 oz pasta (e.g., rotini or penne)
- 1 cup cherry tomatoes, halved
- 1 cup cucumbers, diced
- ½ cup bell peppers, diced
- ¼ cup red onion, diced
- ½ cup Italian dressing
- Salt and pepper to taste
- Fresh basil for garnish (optional)

Instructions

1. Cook pasta according to package instructions; drain and let cool.
2. In a large bowl, combine cooled pasta, cherry tomatoes, cucumbers, bell peppers, and red onion.
3. Drizzle with Italian dressing and season with salt and pepper. Toss to combine. Garnish with fresh basil if desired and serve chilled.

Eggplant Parmesan

Ingredients

- 1 large eggplant, sliced into rounds
- 2 cups marinara sauce
- 1 ½ cups shredded mozzarella cheese
- ½ cup grated Parmesan cheese
- 1 cup breadcrumbs
- 2 eggs, beaten
- Salt and pepper to taste
- Olive oil for frying

Instructions

1. Preheat oven to 375°F (190°C). Sprinkle eggplant slices with salt and let sit for 30 minutes to draw out moisture. Rinse and pat dry.
2. Dredge eggplant slices in beaten eggs and then in breadcrumbs. Heat olive oil in a skillet and fry slices until golden on both sides. Drain on paper towels.
3. In a baking dish, layer marinara sauce, eggplant, mozzarella, and Parmesan. Repeat layers, finishing with cheese on top.
4. Bake for 25-30 minutes until bubbly and golden. Let cool slightly before serving.

Chickpea Salad Sandwich

Ingredients

- 1 can (15 oz) chickpeas, drained and rinsed
- ¼ cup mayonnaise or yogurt
- 1 tablespoon Dijon mustard
- 1 tablespoon lemon juice
- ½ cup celery, diced
- ½ cup red onion, diced
- Salt and pepper to taste
- Bread or wraps for serving

Instructions

1. In a bowl, mash chickpeas with a fork, leaving some whole for texture.
2. Stir in mayonnaise, Dijon mustard, lemon juice, celery, red onion, salt, and pepper until well combined.
3. Serve on bread or in wraps.

Creamy Tomato Soup

Ingredients

- 1 can (28 oz) crushed tomatoes
- 1 onion, diced
- 2 cloves garlic, minced
- 2 cups vegetable broth
- 1 cup heavy cream
- 1 teaspoon Italian seasoning
- Salt and pepper to taste
- Olive oil for cooking

Instructions

1. In a pot, heat olive oil over medium heat. Sauté onion until translucent, about 5 minutes. Add garlic and cook for another minute.
2. Add crushed tomatoes, vegetable broth, Italian seasoning, salt, and pepper. Bring to a boil, then reduce heat and simmer for 15 minutes.
3. Stir in heavy cream and blend until smooth (use an immersion blender or regular blender). Serve warm.

Cauliflower Tacos

Ingredients

- 1 head cauliflower, cut into florets
- 2 tablespoons olive oil
- 1 tablespoon taco seasoning
- 8 corn tortillas
- Toppings: avocado, cilantro, lime wedges, salsa

Instructions

1. Preheat oven to 425°F (220°C). Toss cauliflower florets with olive oil and taco seasoning. Spread on a baking sheet.
2. Roast for 20-25 minutes until golden and tender, tossing halfway through.
3. Warm tortillas and fill with roasted cauliflower. Top with avocado, cilantro, lime juice, and salsa. Serve immediately.

Sweet Potato and Black Bean Chili

Ingredients

- 2 tablespoons olive oil
- 1 onion, diced
- 2 cloves garlic, minced
- 2 medium sweet potatoes, peeled and diced
- 1 can (15 oz) black beans, drained and rinsed
- 1 can (14 oz) diced tomatoes
- 1 cup vegetable broth
- 1 tablespoon chili powder
- 1 teaspoon cumin
- Salt and pepper to taste
- Fresh cilantro for garnish (optional)

Instructions

1. In a large pot, heat olive oil over medium heat. Add onion and garlic, sautéing until onion is translucent, about 5 minutes.
2. Stir in sweet potatoes, black beans, diced tomatoes, vegetable broth, chili powder, cumin, salt, and pepper.
3. Bring to a boil, then reduce heat and simmer for 25-30 minutes, until sweet potatoes are tender. Garnish with cilantro if desired.

Rice and Beans

Ingredients

- 1 cup rice (white or brown)
- 2 cups vegetable broth or water
- 1 can (15 oz) black beans, drained and rinsed
- 1 teaspoon cumin
- 1 teaspoon garlic powder
- Salt and pepper to taste
- Chopped cilantro for garnish (optional)

Instructions

1. Cook rice according to package instructions, using vegetable broth or water.
2. In a saucepan, combine black beans, cumin, garlic powder, salt, and pepper. Heat over medium heat until warmed through.
3. Serve rice topped with black bean mixture and garnish with cilantro if desired.

Spinach and Cheese Stuffed Shells

Ingredients

- 12 jumbo pasta shells
- 2 cups ricotta cheese
- 1 cup spinach, chopped
- 1 cup shredded mozzarella cheese
- ½ cup grated Parmesan cheese
- 2 cups marinara sauce
- Salt and pepper to taste

Instructions

1. Preheat oven to 375°F (190°C). Cook pasta shells according to package instructions; drain.
2. In a bowl, mix ricotta cheese, chopped spinach, half of the mozzarella, Parmesan, salt, and pepper.
3. Fill each shell with the cheese mixture and place in a greased baking dish. Pour marinara sauce over the top and sprinkle with remaining mozzarella.
4. Bake for 25-30 minutes until heated through and cheese is bubbly.

Slaw Tacos

Ingredients

- 8 corn tortillas
- 2 cups coleslaw mix (cabbage and carrots)
- 1 cup cooked protein (e.g., shredded chicken or tofu)
- ¼ cup mayonnaise
- 2 tablespoons lime juice
- Salt and pepper to taste
- Avocado and cilantro for topping (optional)

Instructions

1. In a bowl, combine coleslaw mix, cooked protein, mayonnaise, lime juice, salt, and pepper. Toss to combine.
2. Warm tortillas in a skillet or microwave. Fill each tortilla with the slaw mixture and top with avocado and cilantro if desired.

Roasted Vegetable Quinoa Bowl

Ingredients

- 1 cup quinoa, rinsed
- 2 cups vegetable broth or water
- 2 cups mixed vegetables (e.g., bell peppers, zucchini, carrots)
- 2 tablespoons olive oil
- Salt and pepper to taste
- ½ teaspoon garlic powder
- Fresh herbs for garnish (optional)

Instructions

1. Preheat oven to 400°F (200°C). On a baking sheet, toss mixed vegetables with olive oil, salt, pepper, and garlic powder. Roast for 20-25 minutes until tender.
2. Cook quinoa according to package instructions in vegetable broth or water.
3. Serve quinoa topped with roasted vegetables and garnish with fresh herbs if desired.

Creamy Mushroom Risotto

Ingredients

- 1 cup Arborio rice
- 4 cups vegetable broth
- 1 cup mushrooms, sliced
- 1 onion, diced
- 2 cloves garlic, minced
- ½ cup white wine (optional)
- ½ cup Parmesan cheese
- 2 tablespoons butter
- Salt and pepper to taste
- Fresh parsley for garnish (optional)

Instructions

1. In a saucepan, heat vegetable broth and keep warm. In a large skillet, melt butter over medium heat. Sauté onion and garlic until translucent, about 5 minutes. Add mushrooms and cook until softened.
2. Stir in Arborio rice and cook for 1-2 minutes. If using wine, add it now and cook until absorbed.
3. Gradually add warm broth, one ladle at a time, stirring frequently until absorbed before adding more. Continue until rice is creamy and al dente, about 20 minutes.
4. Stir in Parmesan cheese, salt, and pepper. Garnish with parsley if desired.

Garlic Roasted Chickpeas

Ingredients

- 1 can (15 oz) chickpeas, drained and rinsed
- 2 tablespoons olive oil
- 4 cloves garlic, minced
- 1 teaspoon paprika
- Salt and pepper to taste

Instructions

1. Preheat oven to 400°F (200°C). On a baking sheet, toss chickpeas with olive oil, garlic, paprika, salt, and pepper.
2. Roast for 20-25 minutes until golden and crispy, stirring halfway through. Let cool slightly before serving.

Cabbage Stir-Fry

Ingredients

- 4 cups cabbage, shredded
- 1 cup carrots, julienned
- 1 bell pepper, sliced
- 2 tablespoons soy sauce
- 2 tablespoons olive oil
- 1 teaspoon ginger, minced
- Salt and pepper to taste
- Sesame seeds for garnish (optional)

Instructions

1. In a large skillet or wok, heat olive oil over medium-high heat. Add ginger and sauté for 1 minute.
2. Add cabbage, carrots, and bell pepper, cooking until vegetables are tender, about 5-7 minutes.
3. Stir in soy sauce, salt, and pepper. Cook for an additional 2 minutes. Garnish with sesame seeds if desired.

Beet and Goat Cheese Salad

Ingredients

- 4 cups mixed greens
- 2 medium beets, roasted and sliced
- ½ cup goat cheese, crumbled
- ¼ cup walnuts, toasted
- ¼ cup balsamic vinaigrette

Instructions

1. In a large bowl, combine mixed greens, sliced beets, goat cheese, and walnuts.
2. Drizzle with balsamic vinaigrette and toss gently. Serve immediately.

Cheesy Broccoli Casserole

Ingredients

- 4 cups broccoli florets, steamed
- 1 cup cooked rice
- 1 cup cheddar cheese, shredded
- 1 can (10.5 oz) cream of mushroom soup
- ½ cup milk
- ½ cup breadcrumbs

Instructions

1. Preheat oven to 350°F (175°C). In a large bowl, combine steamed broccoli, rice, cheddar cheese, cream of mushroom soup, and milk.
2. Transfer to a greased baking dish and top with breadcrumbs. Bake for 25-30 minutes until bubbly and golden.

Grilled Cheese with Tomato Soup

Ingredients

- 4 slices of bread
- 4 slices of cheese (e.g., cheddar)
- 2 tablespoons butter
- 1 can (28 oz) crushed tomatoes
- 1 onion, diced
- 2 cloves garlic, minced
- 1 cup vegetable broth
- 1 teaspoon Italian seasoning
- Salt and pepper to taste

Instructions

1. For the soup, in a pot, heat olive oil over medium heat. Sauté onion and garlic until softened. Add crushed tomatoes, vegetable broth, Italian seasoning, salt, and pepper. Simmer for 20 minutes and blend until smooth.
2. For the grilled cheese, heat a skillet over medium heat. Butter one side of each bread slice. Place cheese between two slices, buttered side out. Grill until golden brown on both sides.
3. Serve the grilled cheese with a bowl of tomato soup.

Shrimp and Grits

Ingredients

- 1 cup grits
- 4 cups water or chicken broth
- 1 lb shrimp, peeled and deveined
- 4 slices bacon, chopped
- 2 cloves garlic, minced
- 1 teaspoon paprika
- Salt and pepper to taste
- ¼ cup green onions, chopped

Instructions

1. In a pot, bring water or broth to a boil. Stir in grits and cook according to package instructions until creamy. Season with salt and pepper.
2. In a skillet, cook bacon until crispy. Add garlic and shrimp, cooking until shrimp are pink. Season with paprika, salt, and pepper.
3. Serve shrimp mixture over grits, garnished with green onions.

Veggie Burrito Bowls

Ingredients

- 1 cup cooked brown rice
- 1 can (15 oz) black beans, drained and rinsed
- 1 cup corn (fresh or frozen)
- 1 cup diced tomatoes
- 1 avocado, diced
- 1 teaspoon cumin
- 1 teaspoon chili powder
- Salt and pepper to taste
- Lime wedges for serving

Instructions

1. In a bowl, combine black beans, corn, diced tomatoes, cumin, chili powder, salt, and pepper.
2. To assemble, layer brown rice at the bottom, then top with the bean mixture, avocado, and a squeeze of lime. Serve warm.

Pesto Pasta with Peas

Ingredients

- 8 oz pasta (e.g., fusilli or penne)
- 1 cup peas (fresh or frozen)
- ½ cup pesto
- ¼ cup grated Parmesan cheese
- Salt and pepper to taste

Instructions

1. Cook pasta according to package instructions; add peas during the last 2-3 minutes of cooking. Drain.
2. In a large bowl, combine pasta, peas, pesto, Parmesan cheese, salt, and pepper. Toss to coat and serve warm.

Baked Ratatouille

Ingredients

- 1 zucchini, sliced
- 1 eggplant, diced
- 1 bell pepper, diced
- 1 onion, diced
- 2 cups marinara sauce
- ½ teaspoon dried thyme
- Salt and pepper to taste
- Olive oil for drizzling

Instructions

1. Preheat oven to 375°F (190°C). In a baking dish, layer zucchini, eggplant, bell pepper, and onion. Drizzle with olive oil and season with thyme, salt, and pepper.
2. Pour marinara sauce over the vegetables. Cover with foil and bake for 30-35 minutes until vegetables are tender.

Overnight Oats with Fruits

Ingredients

- 1 cup rolled oats
- 1 cup milk (or plant-based milk)
- 1 tablespoon chia seeds
- 1 tablespoon honey or maple syrup
- 1 cup mixed fruits (e.g., berries, banana slices)
- Nuts or seeds for topping (optional)

Instructions

1. In a jar or bowl, combine oats, milk, chia seeds, and honey. Stir well and refrigerate overnight.
2. In the morning, top with mixed fruits and nuts or seeds before serving.

www.ingramcontent.com/pod-product-compliance
Lightning Source LLC
LaVergne TN
LVHW081333060526
838201LV00055B/2609